To Be Defined

Yanique Renwick

Presentation by *BookLeaf Publishing*

Web: www.bookleafpub.com

E-mail: info@bookleafpub.com

ISBN: 9789357440462

First edition 2023

*I dedicate this book to anyone who can find
healing through my poetry.*

PREFACE

After the publication of my first anthology, readers asked if there would be a part two. I was unable to give a concrete response at the time. Life is a continuation, as is this book. Still aiming to inspire others to become the best version of themselves, while I do the same. Keep in mind that life is on-the-job training, so were allowed to make mistakes.

A Love Letter to Poetry

The sweet sounds of similes
 taste delicious
as they roll off my tongue onto your ears
I can smell the success that is near
I got my senses in a bind
Binding these stanzas together,
Creating a marriage with these metaphors.
I meant it when I said I love you.
She says if it doesn't make money it won't make
sense.
I know there are essentials
Like happiness, joy, and glee.
Yes, I know these are just synonyms
But who's to say,
these feelings shouldn't matter to me?
A happy spouse makes a happy house
Poetry and I have been loving one another for
half my life.
I've said it once and I'll say it again
What every healthy relationship is loyalty
Especially with something that makes me feel
free in a world
 with so many different forms of captivity.
So in spite of what the senses say,
I can hear hues,

and similes sound scrumptious as they roll off
my tongue onto your ears.
Poetry saved me. I love you, baby!

Be a Queen

Act your age,
        Act your wage,
Be conscious of how you carry yourself
        Head up high
            Crown Straight
                Feet planted at all times
This is what it means to be a queen.
Dad always taught me books before boys
because boys bring babies.
Now I'm in the field with a degree
Because education has always been implanted in
me.
They say, what is a queen without her king?
I say, historically, more powerful
Women tend to have the highest graduation rate
Yet have to fight to get a raise, that's a trend on
your graph paper, I see
Through the glass ceiling,
We deserve healing,
At times we need to reparent ourselves,
Dad's saying got me through school.
But what am I to do, about my womanhood?
Because there are white men in office making
laws about my black womb.

Seems to be America has short-term memory
loss.
Maybe that's why it keeps re-re-repeating itself
(GASP)
Uh oh, corporate America heard me Stutter,
Now they say, although I exceed all
qualifications, may be unfit for the job.
Which in turn, makes me sob.
But then I remember,
          Head up high
                    Crown Straight
                              Feet planted at all times
This is what it means to be a Queen.
I took notes from Ms. Neffertiti
And although this rejection may feel like a curse
I know, that things are not always what they
seem,
So I remember to
BE A QUEEN

Call me...

I find myself reflecting on my name,
the same name I used to hate.
All because one teacher couldn't fix his tongue
to get it right.
But now I write.
I write for the younger version of me,
Who couldn't see the beauty in she
constantly hearing the mispronunciation of what
people don't initially see.
Her uniqueness,
Finding shame where it should never exist is a
magic trick.
Call me a magician then.
Finding limits where they don't exist
 those are beliefs
Instilled in me
Subconsciously.
Now i'm working to rewire my brain
Wish I put a special request to my neurosurgeon
to do this for me.
Though I never really liked people doing things
for me.
Asking for help has always been hard.
I never yearned to look weak

There was always a part of me that associated
weakness with help.
 I need more rewiring
Call me an electrician of the subconscious
I've been told I should be a therapist,
But when I go to sleep all I see is poetry
I'm living the dream.
Call me…. a poet

Trip

I've always been naturally clever,
and clumsy
so it makes sense I have concerns about tripping
over my words.
In conversation sometimes i sutter
I've found that's a defense mechanism
from so often not being heard the first time.
I've always wanted a love that's all mine.
It took so long for me to see that love was inside
of me this whole time.
Having trust issues with no one but myself.
Forgiving myself was a long a tedious process,
For giving me the love I so badly craved from
others never did save the who I was.
That's for the best cuz
she died a long time ago
I am now Yanique 3.0
then grow to 4.0
because I'm leveling up like a GPA.
Those who wanted me to stay stagnant have no
place in my life
My cut off game is as sharp as a knife.
As a surgery success story,
I see that even the closest parts of you
sometimes need to be served.

So you can level up
like a Ciara song.
Now transformation begins in
5 4 3 2 1
LETS GO.

Art Project

Hoping they were more than just art for each
other,
more than muse for a muse,
more than a follow for a follow.
This virtual world can make situations cloudy.
Now skies are gray, not even partly sunny,
that could cause clarity.
We all know that the best way to take advantage
of some is to make them confused.
Too busy trying to figure it out
she can't see what's really happening.
All she knows is this math aint mathing.
and she can't compute,
because she won't compete
for a seat at a table that clearly wasn't made for
her.
All she asks is not to become another one of his
art projects.
She's been in too many instances where people
made her feel like a project,
instead of a person.
She wants someone who sees her stripped naked
of all the metaphors and similes and still loves
her like the first day of summer.

Where she can bloom into all that she is
supposed to be.
She needs a gardener
who can pour life into her.

Mixed Signals

There's a reason traffic lights sync up.
To minimize the chance of accidents.
which is the exact reason why Ineed your signals
to sync up.
hoping I don't accidentally fall in love
it's not so much the fall i'm afraid of,
but what will happen once i touchdown.
Will you be there to catch me or
Will I end up with a mouth full of soil and
Manure?
 because this situationship is full of shit.
I've never liked mixed signals.
in the words of Katy Perry,
you're hot and you're cold, you're yes then you're
no.
you're in then you're out
I wish I knew if you were going to stay or go.
because I don't have time for these childish
games.
we're both too old to play
trouble.
so sorry, not sorry,
I just want to connect the dots so this game of
heart twister can be over.
Sounds like I'm asking too much of you.
So how about you dare to tell the truth.

My City

I'm in a toxic relationship.
It's a love hate cruelty
a give and take ambiguity,
like I give you my heart and you give me your
potholes,
i mean graves,
cuz damn them things 6 feet deep
on some social distancing news.
We just tryna cruise down the road
but it feels like a roller coaster.
Take me to the cyclone.
You show me there's a thin line between love
and hate.
Finding someone to date who lives in a different
borough is a long distance relationship. Tryna
make it work so,
MTA... this one's for you:
All the silly rabbits have a fear of fares which
makes us do a hop skip and a jump over these
turning styles. But for us shorter people it's
definitely duck season. When your not too porky
you can fit between bars in order to avoid these
pigs
All this to get my bacon egg and cheese from
Colfax Famous Deli

Meet me out in Queens.
because that's where royalty resides,
hence me.
So you see I'm in this toxic relationship with my
city.
She loves me sometimes though.
Gave me this empire state of mind
so i can see all of the lights in here baby!
and i can be unbreakable like an Alicia Keys
song
Cuz like they say,
If you can make it here you can make it
anywhere.
But in the meantime I'm making, sculpturing,
and building my dreams right here in NYC
 because something every healthy relationship
needs is loyalty.
until I decide it's time for me to
get that that bread
that head, I mean knowledge
and leave.
PEACE OUT

Long Distance Lover

We gave birth to something beautiful
This is a different type of intimacy
One where I know you can feel me,
without the cruch of touch.
We are close , without being anywhere near each
other
because energy has no bounds.
When these mounds of words are able to turn
mountains into mole hills
I feel safe.
You know I can be an over thinker
But when i see your flashing blinker,
I know where to turn next.
You are a leader.
I am too,
I'm just glad we don't bump heads
cuz the last thing I want to do is cause an
accident.
Luckily, we don't believe in those.
So I have a question to pose
May I give you this rose? 🌹
You deserve flowers too.
This is for you, my LDR boo

Breathe

From noose to knee
How cruel can you be?
Slaughter us in the street
this is what I see.
my brothers saying "I can't breathe!"
Strange fruit hanging from the top of trees
Where we'll dry us like a raisin in the sun.
So tell me what can be done ?
My mother thinks I'm going to have a son.
This terrifies me,
because the powers that be,
decide whether or not he gets to live past age 14.
having to teach him existing while black is a
crime.
and they tend to confuse Ids with weapons
because they identify you as a weapon.
So don't be surprised when they call you a thug
for wearing a duie, or sneakers, or hoodie.
Moral of the story:
It's not about the clothes.
it's about the one thing you can never take off.
violence even took my mans take off.
cuz someone let that bullet take off,
right into his soul.

I can't even conceptualize
how someone could be so cold
Guaranteeing the line "we weren't supposed to
get past 25" in bold.
Is that what they taught you up there on the
caucasus mountains?
how to be the Grinch who stole life.
I'm going to teach my sonshine
to always stay bright.
Light is the only thing that drives out darkness.
and yet you are both.
Black people are the biggest paradoxes.
being of light and dark simultaneously.
So if I educate you about the value of our
melanin,
Will you finally let us breathe?

Honesty Hour

I want to write.
I want to write a very honest poem.
somewhere I can pour my heart and soul onto
this page.
Writing the things I'm too afraid
 to hear out loud.
Hearing, making it real.
Allowed myself to remember,
The first step to solving a problem is
recognizing its existence.
So, I want to write.
I want to write a poem
And I feel the need to disclaim
That I feel ashamed
I have been going backward.
I know growth isn't a straight path
So I try not to be so hard on myself.
growth looks more like a trend line in the stock
market.
buying at my lows means investing I myself.
who woulda thought my past forex-perience
would quadruple my life lessons.
instead of rising up like dow jones
when my sis passes me the splif to get stoned
I say yes.

This is not the high I was reaching for.
Desiring to naturally elevate.
I promise this poem is not self hate,
but if I can encourage my mate to skate into
2023 with a fiery tenacity for victory then I
should do that for me.
maybe being hard on myself is in fact the
answer.

2019 movie reflections

I've gotten too far only to get this far
I've gotten too far only to get this far.
I've gotten too far only to get this far!
Imagine me,
running a MARATHON
 Forgetting the reason why I hold on.
Thoughts of "would everyone just be better off"
without me"
so you see, there was a point in time I was
suicidal.
when I wanted to put a point in time and end it,
period.
feeling like this run-on of a life sentence was too
long.
He made emotions my kryptonite
and with every tear shed the fleeting thoughts of
what it would be like if I were dead came to my
head
the overwhelm overtaking me
just as he did my body.
So I find myself taking these moments piecing
them together, like a movie scene
 I watch on the screen of my life.
My life, now
is the light at the end of the tunnel

that she so badly needed to see.
Referring to my past self as she
because I no longer identify with the killmonger
version of myself.
I just want to squeeze all of that sadness out of
her.
But since I had no one to hug me,
I went to therapy
where we would watch the movie scenes of my
life
and dissect the trauma
so I could see the triumph.

Dear young Yani

I know your differences often leave you
ostracized.
sticking out like a sore thumb and I know it
hurts.
The way they taunt you.
All it does is haunt you and I know you've
thought about becoming a ghost because you
don't fit in with most,
but baby girl this test will become your
testimony!
so just keep pushing.
So you go,
you have trouble saying no
cuz people pleasing is the name of the game.
 Fully aware of what you're doing, but you don't
care,
just trying to avoid a snare.
but this turns you into a leaky battery.
becoming more and more drained while just
trying to stay sane.
My advice: Transform the people-pleasing into
protecting your peace.
So you search for a safe space.
Hoping that can become your favorite place.
Never forget

I love you.
You want to be a dancer again.
yet mom says, "not until you do your exercises."
Little does she know, dance is the exercise I've
been looking for and those leg lifts are such a
bore.
I mean, even just a walk to the store is exercise!
this is me trying to justify my lack of movement.
But one day...
you pick up a pen and paper
and now you're a published poet.
Never stoic when you step on that stage
Knowing when it's time to flip the page,
People feel you.
So never forget, I love you.

Black Holes

As black women,
we don't take things lightly.
We take them as they're given.
Giving us the weight of the world and expecting
us to carry it.
Without being phased by the pressure,
That chip on my shoulder is a boulder of
emotion
And when it resonates in my body I feel it in my
gut.
Ladies, this is why we need to trust our gut!
We need to trust our intuition
we are psychic beings,
But society tells us this is mythological
So we don't believe it
We don't believe in ourselves.
When our bodies tell us we can't take this
pressure anymore,
We don't believe it.
Yes, we are black women,
But we are not black holes
We can't absorb everything and expect to be the
same
And I know it sounds cliche,
But it's ok to not be okay.

Though we are rarely reminded of that.
So we allow them to take from us.
Take our smiles, take our attention, take our
control.
We need to take back control!
Because we are not black holes.

Seashells

Sally sells seashells by the seashore
Sally sells seashells by the seashore
Sally sells seashells by the seashore

Someone once compared my hand to a seashell.
It's ironic that the beach has always been my
sanctuary.
  When I laid on the operating table awaiting
anesthesia to knock me out
My mother held my fist and I asked her,
If I wake up when the doctors are done playing
with my brain can we go to the beach and collect
seashells?
Before answering my question,
She corrected my language from the doubt the
devil tried to plant in me.
To grow my certainty she said "When you wake
up"
And now I'm alive to tell the story
of when mom and I went to the beach
specifically to search for seashells.

Superhero

Always taught me not to be a friend feen,
mamma,
showed me what it means to be a black queen,
mamma,
seeing the struggles of single motherhood
strengthen you
YOU ARE MY SUPERHERO
No, you don't have X-ray vision, but you've
always had eyes in the back of your head.
Took that sight and turned it into a vision of a
better life for us.
You showed me what it means to be a psychic
being,
AKA a woman.
Intuition is your power and the feeling is truly
the secret, you can feel what's going to happen
next.
A fortune teller.
You have made me fortunate.
Because YOU ARE MY SUPERHERO
When the deeds you do don't add up to zero,
It's what's inside that counts,
ask any war hero.
such as yourself

cuz I know you've fought battles for me that I
don't even know about.
From custody battles to threatening to take your
own life if those doctors didn't help me!
You've convinced me that becoming a mother
makes you a little "crazy"
but maybe that's what Beyoncé was referring to
when she said crazy in love.
I will never know what that love feels like until I
have children of my own.
They will be so lucky because I have the BEST
example of what it means to be a mother.
mamma,
YOU,
ARE MY SUPERHERO

The St. Albans Parrot

I love hearing you first in the morning.
I meditate to the sound of your singing
What a breathtaking being you are.
I love how free you choose to be
Soaring over my head reminds me, that some
things are above me.
So I should let it go.
Thank you for keeping me grounded once I see
you land so gracefully.
Your green body is so bright, no one can miss
you.
I see you putting your nest together at the top of
light poles.
Reminding me to always stay bright and hold it
together
just as your nest does.

Feeling Divine

Trying to make sure this is real rap
and none of the cap-ricorn
when I think "sink," I think you
calling me boo n that's not usually something I
allow so soon,
but this is different.
1200 miles away, they say long distance doesn't
work,
but beating the odds is kinda our thing.
Now I'm dreaming of you.
So does that mean you're the man of my dreams?
All in my REM because you are a gem.
Yet, you don't want to be a diamond everyone
can see through.
But, transparency is exactly what we need.
I want you to continue to feed my mind
cuz this Sapiosexual has something for you and
those are free-flowing feelings.
They apparently do make Pepto for feelings n
now I feel absolutely divine.

Spelling with Words

I am grateful
I am energetic
I am abundant
I am powerful
I am one with nature.
We're like aloe leaf
Even after the outside protective layer shrivels
up
the inside remains the same.
 When our bodies shrivel up after life, our
inside,
Our souls will still remain the same.
Our spirit lives on because energy can not be
created or destroyed.
I watched the sunset
Focused on the big ball of energy in the sky.
A Magnificent sight.
What a wonder it is to be here with such cosmic
beauty.
in the sun, I feel as one
I am energy too.
The color of my aura is blue
I enjoy helping others, for the law of
transmutation accrues.
Helping those who need it

inspires others to do the same. Let my good
vibrations transfer to you.
This energy can not be created nor destroyed but
it sure can be transferred.
So be careful what you say and who you listen
to.
And repeat these affirmations:
I am grateful
I am energetic
I am abundant
I am powerful
I am one with nature.